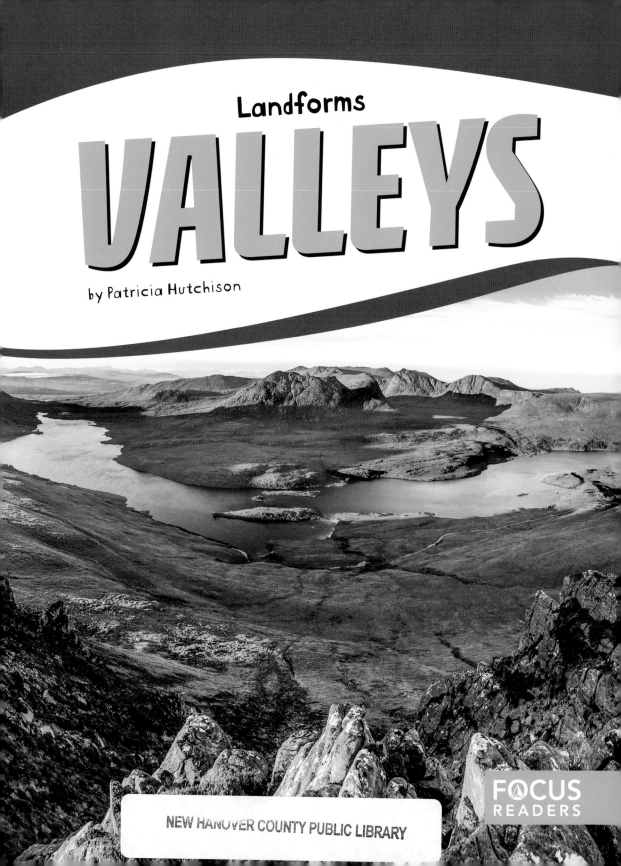

Landforms

VALLEYS

by Patricia Hutchison

FOCUS READERS

FOCUS READERS

www.focusreaders.com

Focus Readers is distributed by North Star Editions:
sales@northstareditions.com | 888-417-0195

Produced for Focus Readers by Red Line Editorial.

Photographs ©: fotoVoyager/iStockphoto, cover, 1; James Whitlock/Shutterstock Images, 4–5; Ami Parikh/Shutterstock Images, 7, 29; khlongwangchao/Shutterstock Images, 8–9; Simon Dannhauer/Shutterstock Images, 11; ArCaLu/Shutterstock Images, 13; kavram/Shutterstock Images, 14–15; Tanja_G/Shutterstock Images, 16; Filipe Frazao/Shutterstock Images, 19; Frontpage/Shutterstock Images, 20–21; Tim Stirling/Shutterstock Images, 22–23; Travel Stock/Shutterstock Images, 24; John Bill/Shutterstock Images, 26

ISBN
978-1-63517-897-5 (hardcover)
978-1-63517-998-9 (paperback)
978-1-64185-201-2 (ebook pdf)
978-1-64185-100-8 (hosted ebook)

Library of Congress Control Number: 2018931697

Printed in the United States of America
Mankato, MN
May, 2018

About the Author

Patricia Hutchison is a former teacher. She loves to research new topics. Patricia is the author of over 20 nonfiction books about science and social studies. When she is not writing, she likes to explore new places while traveling with her family.

TABLE OF CONTENTS

CHAPTER 1

LAND BETWEEN THE HILLS

Snow covers the tops of two steep hills. The rocky land slopes down to a river. The river rolls over rocks. It flows down the hill, carving out a V-shape. Grass grows in the dark soil. This flat bottom is a valley.

A river runs down from snowy Mount Cook in New Zealand.

A valley is a low area of land. This land is often between mountains or hills. Usually a river or stream runs through a valley. All valleys take the shape of a V or a U.

Valleys are found on all the **continents** on Earth. They also exist on the ocean floor. There are

FUN FACT

If a river valley becomes very deep, it is sometimes called a canyon or a gorge.

The town of Banff is located in a valley in the Rocky Mountains of Canada.

several kinds of valleys. Each type

is formed in a different way.

CHAPTER 2

FORMING A VALLEY

Some valleys are V-shaped. These valleys are narrow. They have steep sides. V-shaped valleys are formed by rivers. Many rivers begin on mountaintops. Snow melts, and water flows downhill.

 The Karakoram mountain range in Pakistan has a V-shaped valley from the Indus River.

As it flows, the water **erodes** the rock. Slowly, a V-shape forms between the hills. This process takes millions of years.

Some valleys are U-shaped. These valleys form in very cold mountain **climates**. The snow on the mountains melts in the summer.

FUN FACT

Water flows fastest down steep mountains. The faster the water flows, the deeper the valley it makes.

 The Aletsch Glacier cuts a U-shaped valley through the Alps in Switzerland.

During the winter months, it freezes again. This process happens over and over. It forms a huge chunk of ice called a glacier. It takes thousands of years for a glacier to form. Then, the glacier creeps slowly down the mountainside.

As it moves, the heavy ice grinds away the rock. When the glacier melts, a U-shaped valley is left behind. This type of valley has a curved bottom and steep sides.

Earth's crust is made up of huge pieces of rock. These pieces are called tectonic plates. They are always moving. But they move

FUN FACT

The bottom of the sea has many rift valleys.

The Great Rift Valley in Africa is approximately 4,000 miles (6,400 km) long.

very slowly. When two plates move apart, **molten** rock comes out between them. This rock hardens when it cools. New, flat land forms between the plates. This land is a rift valley.

CHAPTER 3

VALLEYS CHANGE

River valleys begin as narrow paths through the mountains. The moving water cuts into the rock. The water carries away **sediment** as it moves. Much of this sediment ends up in the valley.

 The sediment carried by rivers often makes river valleys good for farming.

 The twists and turns of the Unica River can be seen in the trees even when the valley floods.

Over time, soft soil builds up along the river's banks. Sometimes the river flows over its banks. This process is called flooding. The floodwater eventually goes away. But the soil stays behind.

This process makes the river wider, too. Water in wide rivers moves more slowly. And slower water causes less erosion at the river's bottom.

Instead, the water grinds into the soft soil at the river's sides. One side might erode faster. If that side caves in, water moves in and sweeps away the loose dirt. On the other side, the water moves slowly.

It can't carry the sediment. So it builds up. The new land forms a bend in the river. This process takes many years. It happens at different places along the river's path. In time, the river zigzags back and forth. Over many years, the valley becomes flatter and wider.

FUN FACT

Sometimes a river's zigzags begin to touch. Soil builds up where they touch. It separates one bend from the river. The bend becomes an oxbow lake.

The Amazon River has many zigzags.

THE NILE RIVER VALLEY

The Nile River is one of the longest rivers in the world. It flows more than 4,200 miles (6,800 km) through Africa. The river floods for at least six months every year. Water covers the Nile River valley. It leaves behind a rich layer of soil.

Long ago, farmers learned how to use this pattern to grow crops. They dug **ditches** near the Nile. These ditches moved water into their fields. They grew wheat and cotton.

Many cities that were built along the Nile River long ago are still there today.

CHAPTER 4

LIFE IN THE VALLEY

A river flowing through a valley deposits sediment. **Silt** and clay build up over many years. The soil in a valley contains **minerals** from the eroded rocks. This makes the soil there good for growing grass.

Moose can be found in the valleys of Grand Teton National Park.

African fish eagles hunt in the waters of the Great Rift Valley.

The grass supplies food for animals that live there. Otters, beavers, and deer all live in valleys.

Fish, frogs, and snakes live in a valley's river and nearby streams. Meat-eating birds such as eagles feed on these creatures. Worms and insects live in the soil. They are food for birds such as crows, robins, and blue jays.

The fertile valley soil is good for growing crops. Farmers plant corn, wheat, and soybeans. They also grow hay for cattle and sheep.

FUN FACT

Soil is formed when rocks are broken down by wind, water, or ice.

In Vietnam, farmers build terraces into the river valleys for growing rice.

Some farmers grow grapes and
berries in rich valley soil.

The soil in valleys supports many kinds of life. Without this soil, there would be few plants. And without plants, animals would not survive. Food from plants supplies many things with the energy they need to live. For this reason, valleys are an important landform.

FUN FACT

Researchers believe that people have been farming rice in the Yangtze River valley for at least 8,000 years.

FOCUS ON
VALLEYS

Write your answers on a separate piece of paper.

1. Write a letter to a friend explaining how rift valleys form.

2. Which type of valley would you like to visit? Why?

3. Which type of valley is formed by glaciers?

    A. V-shaped valley

    B. U-shaped valley

    C. rift valley

4. How are rift valleys different from V-shaped and U-shaped valleys?

    A. There are no rocks in a rift valley.

    B. Rift valleys are not formed by erosion.

    C. Animals cannot live in rift valleys.

5. What does **fertile** mean in this book?

*The **fertile** valley soil is good for growing crops. Farmers plant corn, wheat, and soybeans.*

    A. able to grow many plants

    B. able to destroy many seeds

    C. able to cover large areas

6. What does **survive** mean in this book?

*And without plants, animals would not **survive**. Food from plants supplies many things with the energy they need to live.*

    A. see

    B. breathe

    C. live

Answer key on page 32.

GLOSSARY

climates
The average weather conditions of particular places or regions.

continents
The seven large pieces of land on Earth.

ditches
Long, narrow paths dug into the ground.

erodes
Wears something away slowly over time.

minerals
Substances that are naturally formed under the ground.

molten
Melted by intense heat.

sediment
Stones, sand, or other materials that are carried by flowing water, wind, or ice.

silt
Very fine soil that does not have much clay.

TO LEARN MORE

BOOKS

Hyde, Natalie. *Earth's Landforms and Bodies of Water.* New York: Crabtree Publishing, 2016.

Labrecque, Ellen. *Valleys.* New York: Heinemann Library, 2015.

Lindeen, Mary. *Landforms.* Chicago: Norwood House, 2017.

NOTE TO EDUCATORS

Visit **www.focusreaders.com** to find lesson plans, activities, links, and other resources related to this title.

INDEX

Answer Key: 1. Answers will vary; **2.** Answers will vary; **3.** B; **4.** B; **5.** A; **6.** C